I am Sacagawea

BRAD MELTZER

illustrated by Christopher Eliopoulos

 DIAL BOOKS FOR YOUNG READERS

I am **Sacagawea.**

What do people expect of you?

Your family, your teachers, your friends—do they expect you to be a good person? To do well in school? To keep your room clean?

People had different expectations of me.

In fact, they didn't expect much at all.

Why?

It was a different time in America. Back then, they didn't think much of people who looked like me.

Someone who was a girl.

Someone who was young.

Someone who was Native American.

WHEN I WAS BORN, THE UNITED STATES WAS STILL A BRAND-NEW COUNTRY.

GEORGE WASHINGTON WAS JUST BECOMING PRESIDENT.

BUT MY PEOPLE— MY TRIBE, WHICH WAS CALLED THE SHOSHONI—HAD ALREADY LIVED HERE FOR THOUSANDS OF YEARS.

When winter came, the women of our village would pack up our lodges, our homes made of brush we lived in during certain times of the year.

In spring and summer, the whole village would move to an area where there was better fishing; in fall or winter, we moved to different areas for different food.

At the time, I was pregnant. When the baby came,
it would be hard to travel.
But I didn't have a choice.
That's how things were back then.
Besides, Lewis and Clark had a mission...

A mission from President Thomas Jefferson.

But the only way to make it happen was with a translator who could help speak to the Native Americans who were already living there.

IT WAS HARDER THAN YOU THINK.

TO TALK TO A NATIVE AMERICAN, I WOULD TRANSLATE WHAT THEY SAID INTO HIDATSA, A TRIBAL LANGUAGE THAT MY HUSBAND SPOKE.

THEN, SINCE HE DIDN'T SPEAK ENGLISH, HE WOULD TRANSLATE THE HIDATSA INTO FRENCH.

THEN, A MEMBER OF THE TEAM WOULD TRANSLATE THE FRENCH INTO ENGLISH FOR CAPTAINS LEWIS AND CLARK.

WHAT DID HE SAY?

HE WISHES YOU HARMONY ON YOUR JOURNEY.

SHOSHONI, THEN
HIDATSA, THEN
FRENCH, THEN
ENGLISH

By the time we were ready to leave, my son was born. Clark gave him the nickname "Pomp," after a Roman general. It was meant as a joke, like calling a child "Commander." Was it dangerous to take a newborn baby into the wilderness? Of course it was. But we didn't have a choice. I wasn't even considered an equal part of the team. That's how things were back then.

In April 1805, the Corps of Discovery set out from my village to explore this great uncharted land.

Lewis and Clark thought it would be a one-year trip.
They had no idea what they were getting into.

Today, people say I was a guide.
But my real job was as an interpreter.
Soon enough, though, Lewis and Clark realized I had many other skills.

My people lived on this land. I knew its secrets.

With a sharp stick, I'd find wild artichokes that mice had buried in the ground.

It wasn't just food, though.
This was *my* land. My people lived here for centuries.
I understood its passageways.

In their journals, Lewis and Clark spelled my name eight different ways: Sahkahgarwea, Sahcahgagwea, Sarcargahwea, Sahcahgahweah, Sahcahgahwea, Sahcahgarweah, Sahcargarweah, and Sahcahgar Wea. Sometimes, they called me "Snake Woman" or "Bird Woman." But over time, they learned exactly who I was.

In the middle of this pioneering journey, our supplies—which could not be replaced and were needed for our survival—were about to be lost.

Only one person stayed calm.

Carefully balancing myself—with my infant son strapped to my back—in a boat that was about to flip—I was the one who gathered all our supplies.

And all the while, I also did my job as an interpreter, helping Lewis and Clark speak to other tribes.

In Shoshoni, we say you are not human until you learn your language.

These are some of the real words from my tribe:

The Shoshoni word for
Tree is SOHO'BI.

The word for
Corn is HA'NIIBE.

The word for
Water is BAA'.

And the word for
Horse is BUNGU.

There are no words for *Hello* or *Good-bye*.

We don't want to say good-bye forever. So we say something that is closer to "I will see you later."

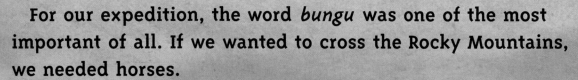

For our expedition, the word *bungu* was one of the most important of all. If we wanted to cross the Rocky Mountains, we needed horses.

Who had them?

The Shoshoni, my tribe.

I led the way.

BE CAREFUL.

THEY MIGHT ATTACK.

I had no idea what to expect that day.

It had been years since I was taken from my tribe.

Our expedition had never seen a Shoshoni war party.
A battle could have started.

But instead of fighting, both sides began to talk.

It was wonderful to see my people again.

We traded with them, giving them supplies and even a medallion from Thomas Jefferson. In return, they gave us horses, helping us prepare for our journey through the mountains.

Eventually, though, it was time to leave.

To this day, no one knows the answer.
Some say it was because we still had more to explore.
Some say it was because I felt like I was part of the team.
Some even say I was inspired by the adventure.
One thing was certain: The mission wasn't done.
So . . . what would you do?

The trip was never easy. We faced grizzly bears.

We were hit by hail and flash floods.

We ate candles to keep from starving. I even got extremely ill.

That winter, our Corps of Discovery had to decide where to build our camp.

Usually, that decision was made by the men in charge.

But for once . . .

WE'D LIKE TO KNOW WHAT YOU THINK.

WE NEED EVERYONE TO VOTE.

INCLUDING ME?

YES, SACAGAWEA.

INCLUDING YOU.

The final decision rested with Lewis and Clark.

But on that day, my vote was cast.

Like everyone else on the team.

Did our expedition ever reach the Pacific?

Yes, it did.

Part of our group hiked to the water earlier than the rest, and sent word back.

THEY SAY THEY SAW A WHALE.

I WANT TO GO.

TO SEE THE WHALE?

NOT JUST THE WHALE.

I wanted to see the ocean, which I'd never seen before.

Eventually, I did.

In the end, our Corps of Discovery traveled over
two thousand miles.
   It took a year and a half—by boat, horse, and foot.
   I was the only girl.
   The only teenager.
   The only one with a baby.

And the only Native American.

In my life, people underestimated me.
Since I was a girl, they expected me to be weak.
Since I was young, they expected me to be inexperienced.
And since I was Native American, they expected to treat me unfairly.
That's how things were back then.
But that's not how they should ever be.

Native American people define themselves by their stories. You know my story now. It's time for you to write *your* story. Don't let someone else limit you.

As Chief Meninock of the Yakama Tribe says: "We can only be what we give ourselves power to be."

Do you know what it means to "navigate" something?
It means finding your way.

Wherever you go in life—
whatever mountains you climb and challenges you face—
find your own way.
Make your own path.
Shatter expectations.

That's what I've always done.
I am a girl. I am a teenager.
I am a mother. I am Native American.
And I am powerful.

I am Sacagawea, and I will blaze my own trail.

"The Indian woman, to whom I ascribe equal fortitude and resolution with any person on board at the time of the accident, caught and preserved most of the light articles which were washed overboard."

—MERIWETHER LEWIS, writing in his journal about Sacagawea after she saved the supplies on the famous boat ride

Statue in
Washington Park
(Portland, Oregon)

Timeline

CIRCA 1789	CIRCA 1800	1803	MAY 14, 1804	NOVEMBER 4, 1804	FEBRUARY 11, 1805
Born in what would later become Idaho	Captured by a rival tribe	The Louisiana Purchase land deal takes place between the U.S. and France	Lewis and Clark's Corps of Discovery departs St. Louis	Meets Lewis and Clark	Gives birth to Jean Baptiste ("Pomp")

A Shoshoni camp in 1870

Sacagawea gold dollar coin

Replicas of canoes from Lewis and Clark's expedition

APRIL 7, 1805	MAY 14 OR 15, 1805	AUGUST 17, 1805	AUGUST 26, 1805	JANUARY 1806	1812	2000
Departs with the expedition from Fort Mandan (North Dakota)	Saves supplies when boat almost tips	Sees her brother, who is now chief	Expedition crosses Continental Divide at Lemhi Pass (Montana/Idaho border)	Sees the Pacific Ocean for the first time	Dies (perhaps) of an unknown illness; never confirmed	Sacagawea dollar coin issued by the U.S. Mint

For Lauri Hornik and Jodi Reamer,
our fearless leaders,
who were there before anyone.
They're the ones who helped us find our way and blazed the trail
that brought these books into existence.
—B.M. & C.E.

Special thanks to Carolyn Gilman and everyone at the National Museum of the American Indian for their input on early drafts.

....

SOURCES

Lewis and Clark: Across the Divide by Carolyn Gilman (Smithsonian, 2003)

Lewis and Clark on the Trail of Discovery: An Interactive History with Removable Artifacts by Rod Gragg (Thomas Nelson, 2003)

The Northern Shoshone by Robert Harry Lowie (Library of Congress, 1909)

"Sacagawea." *UXL Encyclopedia of U.S. History.* Sonia Benson, Daniel E. Brannen Jr., and Rebecca Valentine (UXL, 2009).

"Sacagawea: A Courageous Child Changes History" by Melissa Genzoli, Michelle Thompson, Janet Berg
(*Social Studies Review*, Spring/Summer 2009, Vol. 48, Issue 2, p 50–54)

Sacagawea and the Lewis & Clark Expedition: America's Most Famous Explorers by Charles River Editors (Charles River Editors, 2013)

"Ultimate American History Mystery Woman" by Joyce Badgley Hunsaker (Time.com, July 2002)

Undaunted Courage: Meriwether Lewis, Thomas Jefferson, and the Opening of the American West by
Stephen E. Ambrose (Simon & Schuster, 1997)

Lewis & Clark: The Journey of the Corps of Discovery, a film by Ken Burns (PBS DVD, 2001)

The Lewis and Clark Journals (lewisandclarkjournals.unl.edu)

Sacagawea Historical Society (sacagawea-biography.org)

The Shoshoni Language Project at the University of Utah (shoshoniproject.utah.edu)

FURTHER READING FOR KIDS

Who Was Sacagawea? by Judith Bloom Fradin and Dennis Brindell Fraden (Grosset & Dunlap, 2002)

Sacagawea by Kitson Jazynka (National Geographic, 2015)

Sacajawea: Her True Story by Joyce Milton (Penguin Young Readers, 2001)

....

DIAL BOOKS FOR YOUNG READERS
Penguin Young Readers Group • An imprint of Penguin Random House LLC • 375 Hudson Street, New York, NY 10014

Text copyright © 2017 by Forty-four Steps, Inc. • Illustrations copyright © 2017 by Christopher Eliopoulos

Photo on page 39 of Shoshone camp taken by W. H. Jackson, 1870/National Photo Company Collection, courtesy of the Library of Congress;
coin photo courtesy of the United States Mint; canoe photo © Ron Niebrugge/www.WildNatureImages.com

ISBN 9780525428534 • Printed in China • 10 9 8 7 6 5 4 3 2 1
Designed by Jason Henry • Text set in Triplex • The artwork for this book was created digitally.

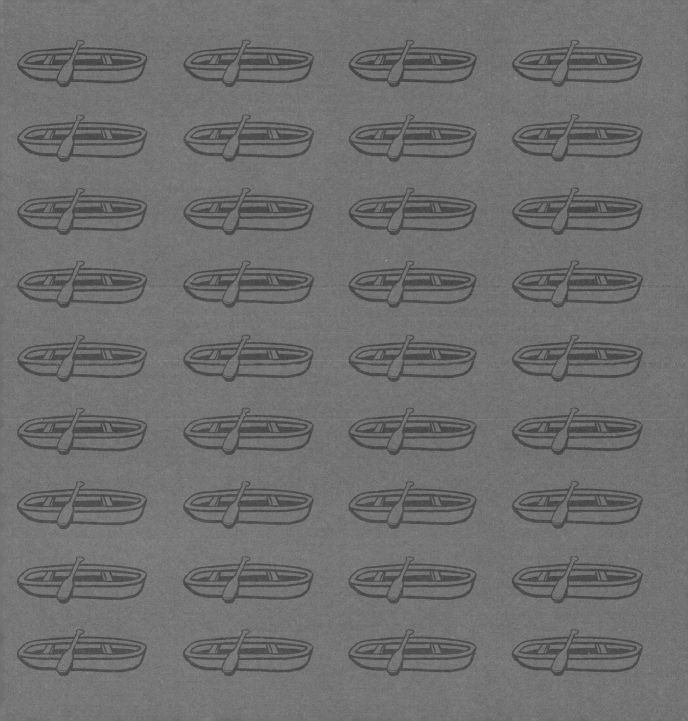